A Joannes Press publication

The Snail and the King © 2024, Norbertine Fathers of Orange Inc.

All rights reserved. This publication may not be reproduced, stored in a retrieval system or transmitted in any form or by any means, without prior written permission of the publisher. Creation, exploitation, and distribution of any unauthorized editions of this work, in any format in existence now or in the future, including but not limited to text, audio and video, is prohibited without the prior written permission of the publisher.

Scripture quotations taken from The Catholic Edition of the Revised Standard Version of the Bible, copyright © 1965, 1966 National Council of the Churches of Christ in the United States of America. Used by permission. All rights reserved worldwide.

ISBN: 978-1-7371230-8-8
Library of Congress Control Number: 2024901347

Printed in the U.S.A.

www.joannespress.com

THE Snail AND THE King

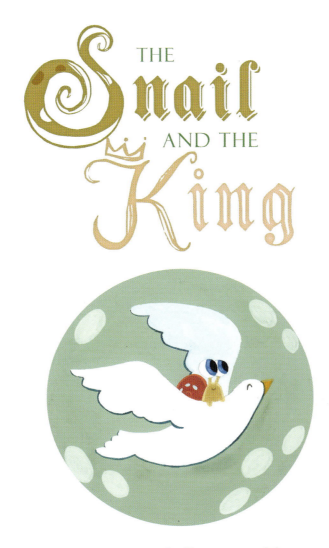

written and illustrated by

Fr. Peregrine Fletcher, O.Praem.

To Andrew, Peter, John and Mary,
with whom I spent my childhood
and with whom I long to spend
eternity.

Once a King sent his own son
Deep into the wild.
He also sent the royal dove
Which flew behind his child.

To all the creatures there
Who, curious, gathered 'round,
He said, "Please come live in our home
Where you'll be safe and sound."

"The wild has been, for you,
A place of fear," he cried.
"With plague as bread and death as bed
And peace you've been denied."

"To get there, you must sail
Beyond the seven seas;
In three days' time, meet on the shore,
But only should you please."

The Prince then showed to all
A map, held in his hand,
So all could find the ship that would
Take them to his land.

Each creature smiled wide
and started on its way.
The journey would be long and hard;
The ship was miles away.

"We are strong and brave,"
The bear said to the horse.
"As am I," the lion roared,
"Now let's begin our course!"

Just then a little snail
Begged from the forest floor:
"Please let me, too; I'll go with you!
I wish to reach the shore!"

They scoffed, they laughed, they jeered:
"You're just a little snail!
Don't make a fuss—the King wants *us*,
And not those who would fail."

And as they walked away,
The snail watched them depart.
"Oh King, I know you want me too,"
He said within his heart.

He set off all alone
And so began his trek.
He trusted in the King's desire
Though sun beat on his neck.

And yet, he didn't burn
For there within the sky
The King's dove blocked the scorching rays
That would have burned him dry.

He trudged along for hours
And came upon the bear
Who, eating honey 'neath a tree,
Had no desire to share.

"Why, bear," began the snail,
"You mustn't stop to snack!
The King will have more food for you,
For nothing does he lack!"

"You preachy bug," groaned bear,
"You'll spoil all my fun.
For in this land there's honeycomb!
What if the King has none?"

The snail made one last plea,
Which greatly vexed the bear,
And then continued on his way
And left him snacking there.

That night a storm rolled in;
A flood was pouring down!
Within his shell the snail escaped,
But feared that he might drown.

Against the rain and wind
His shell could not defend.
But suddenly the dove arrived
To shelter his small friend.

And when the storm had passed,
The snail was still alive!
He went along so grateful that
The dove helped him survive.

Quite soon he saw the horse
Who'd stopped and left the trail.
"Oh horse, we must press on," he said.
"It's nearly time to sail!"

"You foolish little snail,"
The horse neighed with a sneer.
"No more do I believe the King
And so, I'll stay right here!"

"Well, I believe the King,"
The snail said with a cry.
The horse replied: "He won't fool me!
His kingdom is a lie."

He hung his head with grief
As he trudged through the night,
Until he reached a river bank
That filled him with great fright.

He had no strength to cross
And thought he reached his end.
But as tears welled within his eyes,
The white dove did descend.

"Don't cry," exclaimed the bird,
"But climb upon my back.
Allow my wings to be for you
The wings of flight you lack."

So grateful was the snail
As they flew through the sky,
When there among the moon and stars
A sight caught the snail's eye...

"The shore, the shore!" he cried.
"It's time for us to land!"
Right then, the bird, without a word,
Descended to the sand.

The timing was just right
For as the sun arose
It marked the third and final day;
His jouney reached its close!

The snail thanked the King's dove
And crawled to the ship's door,
But stopped because he was alarmed
To hear the lion's roar.

"You made it all this way?"
The lion asked in shock.
"You're so much stronger than I thought
To make it to the dock."

Those words made the snail think
And it became quite clear:
The dove had been there the whole time
To help him persevere.

"I'm here," the snail replied,
"Not by my strength indeed:
The King had sent his dove to me
To help me in my need."

The lion scoffed and said,
"*Alone* I've won this race
And now I know how strong I am
So I won't leave this place."

"For when the ship has sailed
This land will be my own
And I shall rule o'er all who've stayed,
Yes, I and I alone!"

The snail then tried to leave;
The lion blocked his way:
"I order you to serve me in
My Kingdom every day!"

Just then they heard a sound:
An arrow shot with force,
So near the lion that he jumped
And looked to see the source.

It was the King's own son
Who stood with arrow aimed.
"Be gone, lion," was his command.
"By me the snail is claimed!"

The lion leaped away;
The snail approached the Prince
Who said, "I saw you in the wild
And longed to see you since."

"Let's go!" exclaimed the Prince
Who opened the ship's door.
Inside, the snail saw happy folks
Who'd also left the shore.

The ship sailed swiftly towards
The castle of the King.
While on their way they danced and sang—
How could they help but sing?

The lion, horse and bear,
Who chose to stay behind,
All soon discovered they were wrong;
But, by then, the ship was gone—
Too late to change their mind.

And when the ship had docked
The snail became like new!
His shell now gleamed like polished gold,
His spots like gemstones blue.

The Prince then smiled and said,
"Have you now understood?
That here within this glorious land
You are changed for good."

"The light here makes you strong
So that you'll never break.
You'll never cry, nor will you die—
Your heart will never ache!"

The Prince continued on:
"It's time to meet the King!"
The castle doors flung open wide
While bells of joy did ring.

And when the snail arrived
The King took him in hand
And said, "Dear snail, you've traveled long,
Through rain and heat and sand."

"You trusted in my words
And thus I sent you aid:
My own white dove safeguarded you,
My son opened the door for you,
For on my path you stayed."

"And though you suffered much
While on your lonely trail,
At every step you've always been
My own beloved snail."

As for the snail? He *thrived*,
In joy that would not cease;
Forever lived, forever loved,
In never ending peace.

𝕿𝖍𝖊 𝕰𝖓𝖉.

"...but God chose what is foolish in the world to shame the wise, God chose what is weak in the world to shame the strong, God chose what is low and despised in the world, even things that are not, to bring to nothing things that are, so that no human being might boast in the presence of God..."
—1 Corinthians 1:27-31 (RSVCE)

Fr. Peregrine Fletcher is a priest of the Norbertine Fathers of St. Michael's Abbey in Silverado, California. Immersed in a 900-year old tradition, the Norbertine Fathers live a common life of liturgical prayer and care for souls. They also conduct their digital ministry through the Abbot's Circle, a virtual monastery experience of St. Michael's Abbey.

Learn more at www.theabbotscircle.com.